I0145372

Black Raising Cane Over Red

by

Jawanza Dumisani

Glover Lane Press
Publishers Since January 2000
www.gloverlanepress.webs.com

Black Raising Cane Over Red by Jawanza Dumisani
Copyright 2007-2014 by Jawanza Dumisani

ISBN-13: 978-0692227398
ISBN-10: 0692227393

Book cover art provided by Carl Overr
Cover Design by Azaan Kamau
Images Provided by Jawanza Dumisani

All rights reserved, including the right to reproduce or scan this book or portions thereof in any form whatsoever without the prior written permission of Jawanza Dumisani, Azaan Kamau and or Glover Lane Press except where permitted by law. Please do not participate in or encourage piracy of copyrighted materials in violation of author's rights.

The Mission of Glover Lane Press is to Uplift, Empower, Elevate the Masses and Provide American Jobs. Every book published by Glover Lane Press and its many imprints, is printed and manufactured in the United States of America, ensuring and maintaining American employment.

Acknowledgements

The following poems have appeared in various stages of development or versions in print and online or in chapbooks & anthologies.

Beyond The Valley Of The Contemporary Poets, 2002 Anthology

"Muse" (mantra for a poet)

"coal"

Stoetry, Chapbook : FarStarFire Press, March 2003

"Blasphemy," "Empty Graves," "Sammy," "Ben," "Daddy's Epitaph," "Hazelwood Massacre," "coal," "Heat," "Furlough, "Muse, (mantra for a poet)," "Salty," "World News Tonight," "haiku for John," "Statue at Sacred Heart Seminary," "Forgiven," "Case Dismissed," "Happy Dayz,"

"Wife's Council," "Run In With Motown," "love haiku #1," "Brown Baggin'," & "Liberty's Left Hand,"

Speechless, Online Magazine, Winter 2005 "Daddy's Epitaph," & "Blind Sighted,"

City Dialogue, Life During Wartime, Anthology 2006. "Empty Graves,"

"Blasphemy," "Sammy," & "Furlough,"

Voices From Leimert Park, Anthology 2007

"Father's Calling," "Statue At Sacred Heart Seminary,"

Poetic Diversity, Online Magazine April 2009

"House Broken," & " 18 & Over"

Pacific Coast Poetry Series Of Los Angeles Poets Anthology

"Odell's Desire" & "Daddy's Epitaph"

Dedications

This book is dedicated to my late & loving parents Geneva & Roy Dickerson, brothers Eugene, Robert & Alphonso. My late cousin Kofi Lumumba, my late Aunt Annie Battle & Phineas Oliver.

In honor of Billy Higgins, Kamau Daaood and
THE WORLD STAGE for showing us how with our hearts.

Table of Contents

Section III What's Goin On?

Section IV Just Ask The Lonely

Don't Look Back

Mississippi

(1946)

If we never leave
I'd still owe you my life

Regret gnaws
At our future

Wading in power
To dance on water

The meek leap
From river banks

Unborn baptized
Long before my womb

Sharecropper's dream
Turn lonely caregiver

Stumbling over poplar
What ifs & out houses

Steeped in coal & cotton
Colored jus' don't say enough

Unearth secrets transfixed
In the cross's white heat

Chauffeur us down roads
Litter with redemption

Assassinate that ghost
Eavesdropping on our past

Wife's Council

Precious Geneva
vibrato in my song
'r cornucopia spreads north
beyond magnolia's bloom

A harp inside your voice
whispers autumn
Dearest Roy
freedom challenges my tongue
the onslaught recedes

Minin' done robbed us
of earth's last silo
paydays cross-examine
again & again

Two days in Ol' Purgatory
haunts us honey...b' blessed
plant flaming orchids at dawn
leaven 'r days with sons & daughters

sniff the rose, respect its thorn
& finally sit where we please
careful my love,
yo' color has the power to convict

Haiku

fire flies dance bright
Negroes northbound long white lines
cross, rear view in flames

Along The Way

(1946)

strung by sheets
quiet satisfaction,
Bucklow Kincaid hangs

in a well-iron shirt
lie down in green pastures
lodged in a rope

Bessie's blues haunt 'em one by one
her delta moan
soaks the field

Great Grand Ma Short Story #1

damn wretched poplar
candle wax on a letter
white sheets pass by

Head At Mount Glory
Missionary Baptist Church

My bladder eases off the clutch.
Between *Go Down Jericho,* squirt guns
& crescendo of tambourines
pandemonium creeps like a thief.

In the menacing hour of repent
Beelzebub shadows the gates.
"Was that Sister Bell's crème chemise
or Mathew & Luke swapping wives?"

Honey hush,
only thing holding pastor down
is a council of worms
multiplying beneath their sin,
power o' heaven.

"Precious Lord, stitch us
to the under bone of matrimony
or Peter edified without walls."
Crouched over Loretta Kincaid's red sun dress
Deacon Wright's blue serge shimmers.

Sanctuary of secrets
poised at benediction.
All this testifying
got me skimming pennies
for jaw breakers.

Forgiven Was Her Name

snake eyes, crimson & bloodless
dead lovers rise
for one last seance
& you linger

like a war crime
ho' deep & dirty
you squander countless chances
to deliver me

snow blind in June
hung
in slaughterhouse
of denial

my dark joy
whispers Forgiven
& ten red pincers
pierce flesh

your shadow
slips out that red dress
& scarecrows 'cross Winston County
go up in flames

pluck dried lilies
from a sixty-six hearse
yo' mouth spittin' hot gin
in the exit wound you left

love haiku #1

miss you, riding hard
like Shoemaker in the 5th
ball deep in yo' turf

Living For The City

Case Dismissed

(Detroit, 1956)

Cornered by swamp liquor & crushed pride
this peck-a-wood comes to
after smelling salts
& blue arm persuasion
coal miner's scowl

bearing down
like antebellum sun
two stories
Roy Singleton in cuffs

nigga's word don't count no how

Claim he was struck
Once with a hammer
Daddy's third knuckle
still oozing from the blow

haiku for spring

noon's lull from the storm____
　　　　　　　one snail's long journey
　　　　　　　　　　　begins

Great Grand Ma Short Story #2

massa' clears the house
that hound dog buries his nose
spoiled meat 'n the gut

brown baggin'

Momma sends me to school
armed with peanut butter
& jelly sandwiches

wood louses lured by ladybugs
& strumming BB's broom
steer me past trouble

deuce bag shuffle,
carnivores swing
from dope house trees

the monkey's free hand
scrapes maggots from my Converse
before returning

snowdrifts abound
a flyswatter hangs
near the door

sharing a double
Eugene & I
bury secrets between us

he squirms
like an octopus in traffic
daddy chides *give him room*

drunk on dreams
we divide nightmares
fermenting on the porch

Run In With Motown

I take turns hiding childhood
From puberty's key & red women
Swap *Aleda loves* glances
Become a man
Before streetlights flicker

August climbs
Steamy treadmills
Of azure sky
Stars balloon
To crystal balls
Full of dreams

My hands, my hands
Hubcap off '57 T-Bird
Collides with pampered spokes
Of a tenor's chariot
Sleek as distilled water
Do-Do brown Electra
Swerves & brakes
On '63's Good Year

My headstone's chiseled
Pissed as two drunks
Scraping over spilled wine
Levi of The Four Tops
Leaps out, looms over
Like Mount Rushmore
Just Ask The Lonely
Waxing stones

Blind Sighted

Booms Farm Apple on the sly
these b' steamy nights in Détwa
steeped in Mason-Dixon lullabies.
Praise the Lawd'
Bessie's back bendin'
gut bucket hallelujah
hump Tucker twins hollow spine__
Momma say, *les you heathen*
knockin' boots don't feed no mouths.

She's so divine, step solemn
with holy-ghost precision
disciple's revelation hell or shine
Mid June sprinkle plays trashcan song
hawk's eye in every drop.

Soaked to the gristle, Clancy's mutt Luke
showers a basement party; buffalo nickel
taped to everlasting arm
of a broke down phonograph
sanctified by Motown bombs
endowed with power
to keep peace & steam passion.

Barely twelve, country foot taller
I'm gym shoe slick, school yard savvy
her menu regulates my go.
Banana pudding spiked with truth serum,
Sunday spread indentures my tongue.

Six-one tippin' 205
Daddy's leather kisses like a stingray.
Towers in gingham behind Ray Charles eyes,
torches toast when her workload fattens.

Playing house with Nay-Nay swells my shorts.
Angst; noon whistle 'til night shift sleeps
avocado green shag paced Trojan thin
hoping this transgression
don't conjure up his likeness,
pray Ford Motor toils overtime.

Momma four-eleven & eighty pounds shy
her shadow shades Goliath.
Claim God's pet eagle
peers from sacred branch
'top Brother Green's apple tree.
Somehow she kno'
bellyache jus' a few bites
from savored moments.
Seems Reverend Perkins
dun' prayed her to a place
where she could see everythang.
Wish we knew each other
like we did 'n dem days.
Shot marbles & hoops
'stead of Saturday Night Specials.
Ol' Lady Cobb b' yellin'
"Stop dat diggin' dem holes out chere!

Only drive-by was the produce man,
makeshift Huffies, pushcarts
capped with bottle tops & balloons.
Good Humor three-wheel
leanin' slow & greazy
trigger-glad, bells blaring.
Sun-fried faces swarm
like knats to left over lunch in July.

Momma plays half blind,
got 20/20 planted in low brush
at Edgewater Park; bloodhound
'tween sun-sleep & streetlight.
Ten o'clock stare
chases me to bed
& Bloody Bones from nightmares
I'll never dream.

I yank a red wagon
corner to corner, block to block
baggin' empty Faygo Fruit Pops to swap
fuh' two cents each, jumbos five
like that frosty emerald Uptown
Herman tricked Pee-Wee into guzzlin' piss from.

Fo' my feet hit carpet
she drills me 'bout saving
a dime of that dollar
fuh' church on Sunday.
Momma human too
don't see the flame
in my front pocket,
got no idea
how much I've already spent.

Happy Dayz

(long after the French have gone)

Napoleon's ghost rots on St. Helena__
sun up 'til a blind pig sleeps
church folk cut up like Pigmeat.
Night fo' Sabbath young lovers chant
This Old Heart Of Mine
till homing pigeons swoon.
Sam The Sham & The Pharaohs
parody sultans on wax, planets orbit
four fellows from Liverpool
R-E-S-P-E-C-T

Détwa temp-steps Motown
rolls Big Three's tank couture
Motor City copulates to rhythm.
We bathe in Jade East & jazz
wind sobs, ears burn
thank God almighty, free at last.
Yellow jackets draw swabs for blood
Jimi nods *All Along The Watchtower*
when the white boy sits in.

August '69 I parley a hooker's wisdom
into virgin lust on patchwork
'neath vermilion at Edgewater Park,
teenyboppers only smooch.

We shake a tail feather
with two dollar death, play chicken
in traffic on Woodward Avenue
like matadors in Italian knit, silk 'n wool
& spit shined gypsy splits.

Village reveres neon chariots
& high fashion, well-oiled creed lived
among pimps, dope dealers, fugitives & paid killers.

Maybe drunk, but no angry man sets foot
on Ma Ethel's porch & parts the same,
humble spread guarded by mythical lions
honored even by thieves.

School Yard Game

Roughnecks huddle round sawbuck & change
heaped on a hankie, we scoop & scatter.
Somewhere between Econ & English
Sha-Sha wagers a JFK half, pink Bazooka bubble
grease-smeared bangs; laughter
drift into Bumgardner's lab like hyenas.

Roll call remands us one by one.
Earshot near, welfare mama smells dollars
multiply in brain of her fifth, favorite son
father's dark Irish flaw. Hell-hot dice click & rattle
click & rattle like hooker's haunting stroke.
Brick wall bounce keeps us legit, blades buttered.

See-Slick clutches a Jackson from his *Free Press* route.
Hawks trading hand signs signal *coast clear*.
Black cat limps across yard & no one flinches
chalkboard caterwaul, crap game jabber.
Geneva's boy need new shoes...what they hit fo?
New Math & poverty make us cousins.

J&M loafers turnstile in my head
on layaway at JL Hudson's. Clouds vanish
like steam from a manhole; June simmers gray sky
soapbox blue. Dragonfly hovers, hearts pound
six bits of my lunch fare fattens the pot. Stomachs roar,
cafeteria churns out stretched Boyardee.

Jake loops smoke rings as the circle leans in
poot butts bet sunrise he spans a hundred.
Pee-Wee's ancient eyes mirror Pooky's nod
off Chu Lai Trail. In a sleepwalker's trance,
elevens & sevens tumble from labyrinths of light
greenbacks leap like salmon.

Sin-soaked tongues curse boxcars back to back
each pass wails *Jonah repent.*
Deuce bag in PJ's hip whispers my name
First I Look At The Purse
pipes from stereo phony shirts. His last buck
split two ways jump-starts this run.

Outnumbered, we brass knuckled 'r way
down Gladstone alley; him for me, me for him.
Books tallied, kilo of coin bankrolls
a Wall Street swagger, my Levis sag
like Methuselah's nuts. Knocked by the bell,
snakes eyes stare through me
while Momma toils in some white woman's home.

Eighteen & Over

I strut in like a false bottom
at fifteen & a week, bone licked
continental clean. Smitty
nevah' sweats me for ID.

John :Law drops by
I lean back on a cue stick
& hide behind my dead Daddy's frown.
Roll in from English 101
to Nine Ball & 'Trane
steaming out the jukebox,
pass stench of Big Tony's day 'ol stogie
gulp *Faygo Red* 'round yard
of sentimental blue-green slate
'til a mark bites.

Worst thing, its always smoky.
Sho' we cuss like it makes men
as anger swells the chest
of an armchair Ali. Wolf tickets
fisticuffs. Never guns.

Awwww Shit!
Cleophus dun' clammed
on another bet for a fin he ain't got.
Watching him spin his way out an ass whuppin'
is worth the price of his unpaid debt.
Cu-come man,
you kno' a blood bucket can't earn a Lincoln,
slow yo' drag 'til my eagle shakes free.

Every other greeting
a poly-rhythmic nigga'
as Dizzy blows
Wes bumps or Miles is *All Blue.*

Day I turn legal, I stroll in
& flash proof on Smitty.
Ya' lil' som' bitch!
I knew you was a man
moment you set foot in these woods.

Odell's Desire

That Odell is tight as dick's hatband.
Grips a candy red '62 drop-top Caddy
four fingers of Thunderbird boils in the glove,
his basement conk shimmers like onyx.
It's Friday; the eagle's flew,
sports white polyester
like a ticket to heaven.

Seeing his boys grant blessings,
five turn the corner tattered
cardboard to concrete
worn soles flap rhythm he's deaf to.
Daddy, Daddy, give us some money!
Two bits flipped above straw brim's tilt
here, split it & slide as it lands
in dirty palm of 3rd eldest.

The meter's off
& its too hot for hosiery.
Sliced from southern pride's hip
switching hard enough to churn butter
a hooker draped in cheap scarlet
leaks dime store enchantment
down fast lane of his desire.
Hey slim goody, what them draws flop fo'?
"Twelve & three sweetie."
Here's ten in my back seat.

Miz Rodchester feels engine heat; shakes her head,
mutters prayer for those living off their hide
Ol' Lady Cobb peeks from a 2nd floor window
pressing cornstarch into a week's blue collar.

Front end swings into an alley & parks,
King Pleasure serenades her shallow touch
soothes like a phantom mother from his past.
Odell kindles his lust, divides pigeon dung
on a rusty VW, into how many strokes
the flame lasts & picks a Tri-fecta.

What's Going On?

Malcolm's Lament

In '65, gunshots atomic,
Beehive hall in Harlem
Amplified with grief

I'm betrayal
Sin's hurled stone
I know Christ will never save me

He jailhouse juice
Blowtorch in each word
Petty pimp's lost translation

Clutching M1
In shatter-box window
Firebombed dream

Blasphemy

North Star became a swan
Sitting on thirty pieces of silver

A watchdog growls
& ID's real culprit

Scribes hocking redemption
Rush from an unsettled stone

Empty cross, lodged
In tooth for spleen

Loopholes drill for oil, but
There is no lake of fire

Nukes hang
From 1600 Pennsylvania Ave.

Priests coming unto children
Clear their throats

Plump guy in a red suit
In bed with a prophet

Salvation blurred
Between fairytale & thugs

Last Supper
Judas cries out!

Momma Say

There's grace
In forgiveness

I say
No malice
Or clemency
In forgiving
Dead perpetrators
With keys to dreams
Hidden inside
Lucifer shadows

She say
Let us pray

You Slept

(Summer 1968)

Our Lord: The Jaws of Life,
Lay hands on
and speak him home.

Mother___

Infirmed at Mount Carmel ICU
suspended between giant chrome hoops
& the firmament, spouting a litany of tubes
one hundred twenty days after crash.

Dead weight turns, you don't
veins eat, not you; still
your blue dye courses, hands laid on
yearn for our revival.

Anointed with obedience
I oil your black torso
glistening like pharaoh
in July's isolated tomb.

Transcendental vigil
watching you sleep.
At fifteen, I waiver
August sears on.

Kneading your broke body
into autumn's patient arms
exposes the rib's Braille,
thump in a bedpan reassures.

September's middle finger taunts
Science waits hand & foot.
Premonitions chanted in your ear
chaperone my weary prayer.

Bet a Faygo Red you're dreaming
box seats along 3rd baseline,
Momma's onion burgers & fries
hold the government cheese.

Alagae Syrup 'n biscuits
Smokey & The Temps
front row at Motown Revue,
nurse Jenkins honey brown…

Sudden as church bells
opening morning glory
you awoke. Voice box latched
I cherish first hollow whisper.

Eyes lock; corner lost time, jailed stares
wonder where we've been.
Graduation to Welch's communion
your clutch double two days before,

empty space only silence fills.
We spring toward fall's equinox
what we've missed
chronicled on your cast.

It's October Bob
I'd love to stand you up,
brush you back with junk curves
'til streetlights buzz.

Squabble for last hunk
of Aunt Lucille's golden pound,
skate trios to Shorty Long
at Arcadia with you & Al.

Before Seatbelts Were Law

Three years post crash
Sammy careens in a storm
Without an umbrella

At thirteen each game
Kick-starts wheelchair
Pushing skyward

Inch by chromosome
Ghosts arm-wrestle
Another borrowed year

One leg south of sixteen
His riddled arm betrays
Tracks like Northwest Rail

Skull & crossbones
Up tomorrow's sleeve
Grin a savage glare

Wishbones clutching Bibles
Return from another life
Insomnia empties a hole

His shadow's henchmen
Play musical chairs
With the heart's detonator

Eulogy crumpled
Shell game's empty hand
Headstone's threadbare song

Ben

Flesh & metal
Flung skid mark
To concrete wall

Sammy's brother
The only one
To walked away

Slightly grazed
Weeps like war wife
Unaware of time

The guardian of fear
Sets up shop
Cheek refuses to turn

Life flashes slow mo…
Stitching a wound
Going through

Hit & run merges
Amnesia crosses a bridge,
Vanishes beneath the tongue

Deceptive road signs
Look back pointing fingers
Each glass filled with meaning

Mother's boundless hope
Slumbers as eyes flicker
Stranded between God's mercy & Benzedrine

Black Raising Cane Over Red

1. *Color Struck*
Momma cleans houses beyond the city's caged edge.
Grab joy, flag bus, happy Congo Ra Summer. Each fall
Sears *Roebucks* us in, brown canvas jimmies buzzed
through by first snow.
Mississippi thirty-twos tease; gold tooth gleams
as notions clerk needles her stingy tongue.
Arnold Palmer cardigans in carbon colored rows choir
my name. Desire baptizes me red
she plucks it from my eye, *you too dark.*

Line #7 butter-knifes through town
down Tiger Stadium's third base line,
right at Pontchartrain Hotel
pass Capper & Capper's segregated door.
Transfers please.
Driver's Aqua Velva divides our noses
we share his Polack windshield view.
Our commute snags on ruby billboards
Cover Girl sky, Woodward's last mile squirms
like a dry seal. She pans faces for forgiveness
pink mannequins haunt her stares.

Red wagon brimming *Sunday News*
exempts me from cornstarch collar
& Zion's brimstone; blade safe on a promise.
Reverend Perkins looms like a prophecy
I ponder purgatory, tyrannosaurus Rex
paperboy's lake of fire, *delivered.*

Billy club swagger,
back page blues
July burns, my route clears a hundred.
Twenty bones weekly stretches
Momma's elbow grease
ending shame's September ritual.

2. *Love Me Do*
Mirrors despise me
I hop-scotch plantations,
backtrack Jim Crow's holy ghost
kinks tighten like Jackson County noose,
Momma's hot comb gloats & grins.

High yellow cousins on Daddy's side
bask in *we betta' than*. Perm, lock,
plait, burn; twists branded in the heart.
You ain't got good hair. Something withers
with each *you so black...*

Man side of fifteen, Mrs. Kirk
hones my ghetto 101, fairy-taken
to Shakespeare's feast.
Curiosity lights my way,
I savor *Paradise Lost*. From beyond
she ferries me to this radiant moment.
Momma's voice loops *lets us pray*.

3. *Beginning*
In '61 she rebukes scarlet
at The Minor Key. Haloed
in blue smoke & undulating hips
Red Garland stains black ivory rose,
his fingers are angels closing a wound
juke joint & Jesus converge.
Womb water to the cross
cloned as a child should go.
Her rheumatoid resides in me.

Pimped like a barroom whore
comforts the loathsome.
I sift retribution's bowel
smear prayer on wounds
spit out Mother's red phlegm.

A dark room is no hiding place.
Stranded between Nina's four hues
celluloid evicts me frame by frame.
King James pawns my missing grail
The Hidden whispers *here*.

Just Ask The Lonely

Crave

(For Charles Edward)

Hands claw from a crowded grave
tremors flood & wane. In a stupor
Charles Edward wears a sign that reads
don't give up on me.

Held like a grudge, syringes
drain last days from loved ones.
God sends a lifeboat, it returns empty.
One prayer after another
commemorate the faithful
something withers away, the half-dead
shake dust from pinstripes.

At a holiday gathering
rumor & innuendo eavesdrop,
gossip leans in.
Coronaries heaped
on wedge wood in silence.

After Father's funeral
Mother's glare says *I'll sever your feet
to keep you above ground.*
A body bag hangs in her closet.

Desperate, you return one night
to that hollow house in exile
past neighbor's rusting Dodge,
Jimmy Lawhorn embalmed at wheel.

Toe tagged, autopsy states
cause of death : *asphyxiation by lust.*
A bomb ticks in my head. I stand
near a punch bowl, defused.

Haiku (for John)

if heaven were tongues
licking a Coltrane solo
earth should be empty

Coal

Daddy's lungs labor
like one-well town
pink tissue charred & useless
as Ol' Purgatory Mine in W. Virginia

headlamp low,
trapped for two moons
cage of bones
drug out like effigy
before burn

mute as crosses
messiahs in spectacles & white coats
anoint nightstand; yellow
red, fuchsia every four
bright two-tones with meals

tonics, elixirs
& hands laid on
hard one to swallow
horse-size
once a day   everyday

memoir, his body
typeset to scripts
serene as a monk
bedridden on nails

glowworms prey
below headstone
on florescent side
of Wayne County

aorta's lug nut
sheared off
in my hand

Daddy's Epitaph

I

After boot camp, Alphonso your eldest, renamed you
Sir, Kool Menthol & time clocks rigged for spring

Scrawny imposters at Ford Motor, spun from sweat &
steel Cast into men mimicking each drag

Aunt Mariah brands you Congo,
Wandering crusader for lost infidels

Yang of Uncle Simon, a paisley ascot; I wonder
How long ago & which side of the Nile you roamed

We are both distant twins of antiquity. Boxed
in 3 by 6 pantry we dance the ceremony of anger

Yo' cap toe, ham-boned into my hide
Love's unspoken invocation, not a broke dish

Baptized in maid's water, I dip hands to save you
Wash your back, bow my head & pray

Your hand serves righteous discipline
Mine reserved to dignify you

I, 3rd son of blue hurricanes
You, forgotten dynasty of tongues

Architect of my breath
These palms keloid in reverence

Son of an emancipated sharecropper,
Pinned two days inside a mine in West Virginia

Crushed shoulders, coiled spine
 Fallen parishioner, gutted by black lung, dragged

Each holy morning; Royal Crown Pomade,
A stocking cap & one penny crowns you king

I dreaded Sabbath 'til you
Passed out five pennies for the plate

Rev. Perkins swore by a snake in the garden
Secret sentry at door of infidelity

Truth revealed by a close cousin
Only dialect we own

 Forgiveness begged from 7th pew for little more
Greater treasures found in a Naugahyde rocking chair

 You & Mother anchor a sea of sepia
 East mantel an archway

Of our brick two-family flat off West Grade River
Plastic slipcovers, McDonald's first Friday

Powder blue Fairlane rusting in our driveway,
Relic of your phosphorus glow

Last breath stuck in my throat
Ushering earth to swallow you whole

Hazelwood Massacre

Detroit, 1968

Temptation dives toward death
beyond loaded sunsets
down a trapdoor
to rise from oblivion's red teeth.

Coaxed between cross hairs
close enough to belch blood in Technicolor
sniff the high octane of gunfire
pumped through a silencer, ricochets
off each brush with John Law.

Here's Johnny
& seventy-two hours
got me viewing coffins
'stead of cased in one.
Sixty-four pallbearers
year long eulogy.

Silence drips pin-drop murder
badged in to *serve & protect*.
Time clocked from a dead sleep
turnkeys stumble through mug-shot dreams.

Mourning first son's slave-horse vein
Mrs. Hornsworthy declares
*a drug dealer looks best
all stiff & dressed up.*

Dawn microscopes this moment:
the city sleeps like bats.
Tucked in her black C-cup
Geraldine Johnson's food stamps
get trigger punched.

Triple beams click into gear
as Wilbur Grant's last load
clings to Downy's gray static
in dryer at Fresh 'N Clean.

 Motorola lifted from Mr. Dikethrope's den, pawn
ticket buried in lone son's hip pocket stub 666, Swap
Shop's gain; sorrow distills father's filial rage. The
tongue freezes, closes in on his wife's last year.

Mackinaw twins divide three nieces
bury Pearl & spar over wardrobe
to die for; kingpins gloat
in underworld. Spittle eats away
at a newborn's bib.

A whole chicken thaws
in Grace Willard's kitchen sink
while Leon "Smitty" Hobbs alarm
rings 'til Duracell dies,

fear swells like a carbuncle
on widow's bad leg.
Lone survivor's second story leap
lands in bed-stacked asylum.

Throng of flies tremble
no clues & ghost luck take root
corpses slip into halos, secrets
cake in corners of mouths.

Alibis & misdeeds
interrogate the eyes
till it's folklore,
dead man's final breath.

Beneath a star-specked cloak of indigo
sixteen shoes tiptoe into darkness,
from eight pair
tied up in misfortune.

Clothed in patchouli, plumes of cannabis
play possum, masquerading
like a junkie's empty promise.
I slumber under Motor City moonlight
& Momma's Mississippi curfew.

The Chimney

I am done with this dust. I am done.
                    Lucille Clifton__

I

Keloid tracks surround my fifteenth year
apprenticed to four brothers, haberdashers
white powder caked beneath their nails
warn: *Never shoot the monkey.* Midnight

on a roof, two dope fiends plot & scheme
skullduggery every vein. Fox Theater's red neon
freeze-frames each move; no straws drawn,
no coin toss or rock paper scissor.
You county check thin, climb down.

II

Brick mortar wedged
botched break-in
your scrawny cage
foreshadows doom
sack of bones
jam chamber's crown.
Staged like a séance
accomplice seals your tomb.

The Golden Arm
lures broken legs
to war without foxholes.
You survive Vietnam
for Saigon's syringe. Hell
smolders beneath your tongue.

Crow's bate in a crevice
urge to breathe shatters.
Bruised confession
soiled, feathered,
crucifixed & kicking
your waning clock
wails to empty indigo.

III

Day twenty-four June's mercury drive us home
lone vulture tracks Rod & Reggie's reek patrol.
Sprung on coke, elder Calvin scolds young Jerome
"get Pest Pros back on the goddamn phone."

Exterminators search weeks for rat remains 'til a
journeyman sniffs you down, last meal curdles 'round
your dry shell.
Forty days in a chimney
spares my pious skin, rigor mortis creeps
I mock your mute lament.

Time is a wolf pack
courting the graveyard's leer
lifelines migrate into oblivion.
Ice chest for a heart, hinged at the hip
I dance with your cadaver.

IV

Years later in a dream, twelve steps
from where your mausoleum stood
July explodes with a desperate boil
just before coroner pried you from our vise.
Beneath mound of guano, drenched in yellow foam
arresting your infestation. REM morphs to maggots,
hemisphere of flies swarm that empty lot pepper an
azure eclipse, calculate your flesh's journey.

Days after, two mystic birds at my door
pilgrimage back to that rooftop
granting old ashes permission to speak.

V

Anonymity distills grace
my crave vanquished, parched
& embalmed like you.
Buried omen exhumed,
my doppelganger haunts.

The bed I grew up in always needs making.
Caged in a sleepless moon
north pole fetal, bucket of sweat
wooden spoon between my teeth.

Berry's Rhapsody

Its one in the wretched morning
Lovelorn, blue collar weary & booted
His penny pinched shadow
Heaped at big sister's gracious door.
Melancholy & black coffee
Bob & weave like Sugar's prime
Lonely Teardrops cascade
Hound Jackie to wail his pain.

Brown Bomber wannabe: ten & two
Buck forty pounds ring Ebenezer's bell
'Til Draft Board scores TKO,
Korea keeps thirty-two keys intact.
Ain't Too Proud To Beg
Hock Burg-Berry Fund
For eight hundred bones
& a shot at emperor of R&B.

Roll the dice, shadowbox time
Toil 'n sweatshop's wishbone song
Chase two-track dream
Dancing In The Street, five conked heads
Temp-step West Grand Blvd.
Wallowing in a hoosegow's daze
Uncle Lester got sober & saved
When Hitsville moves west.

Red line cages us like mice
Jim Crow hones a switchblade temper,
Clyde Wingate shot over Stetson shine.
Windsor Tunnel to 8 Mile's last loop
Blue Note & Motown scrap for jukebox slots Count
tips in Gordy's favor, birthrate swells Fisticuffs &
stabbings drop Like hooker's drawers in spring
Mulattoes named *Bernadette* potpourri red night air.

Three ghetto girls churned worldly women Serenade
captain's Caribbean port of call.
Baby Love births deadbeat daddies, *Distant Lovers* Scale
Tammy & Marvin's Everest.
Chile bowl pimps eye *My Girl.*
Curfew & tutors in tow, omniscient Mother Up-shifts
Little Wonder's groove

This ain't damn daycare,
Finger Tips in Braille.
Lured to Indiana *Easy As ABC*
Soup bone tender, fleet footed as Georgia Godfather
Michael amp-loads marquee's astral glow, *Got To Be*
There fondles puberty's sweet spot.
Casting lots from wellspring's file
Collective dissects each note,

Caves to *Stubborn Kind Of Fella'*
Nose diving to double plastic
He morphs & ignites the rancorous
Free falling into risky anthems
Father, Father, What's Going On?
It was the 3rd of September.
Jacked by bullets, Malcolm & Martin
Arm wrestle martyred wisdom.

War loops like Krishna benediction
From a bar stool on Five Mile at Mozambique Luc
Kildare somersaults into ditch outside Khe Sanh.
Tanks & green drab swarm Linwood Avenue Lula Mae
Tucker scans battalions
For his carbine stare, discharged in '69
With a spike in his arm, pink hot pants
Turn buck private crimson.

Blind pig on 12th Street
Sparks *Ball Of Confusion.*
Heat Wave gut checks 'r defiant hope
Enshrined in flames, Rare Earth burns.
Holland, Dozier & Holland
We throw up hands & holla'.
Streetwalker's alabaster touch
Whispers under a husband's midnight moan.

Smokey slow drags gold throat's lusty ravine
Innuendo uncoils libidos,
Debutantes tightrope virginity's fault line
Phyllis Latimer's pristine kiss
Singes my adolescent tongue; joystick
Out the hedgerow like *my Momma told me*
This landfill gang plowed & quartered
Into charred lots & rolling stones.

Great Grand Ma Short Story #3

when the whipping cease
lone child up for sale
Freedom gotta' run

Heat Wave

Heat Summer of '68

Route to school turn firestorm.
Crickets don't tap away at silence
& I hear a trapped dog howl
as Linwood Avenue burns
in the shape of a benediction,
rooftops swivel like turrets.

Tear gas seeps through anthills
'til Grand Ma hallucinates cotton bowls.
Elms wither; apple tree's bounty
shriveled as aged beauty, cider
& homemade pies deferred
soot 'cept where tires rest.

Gangrene ferments to rage:
Panthers proclaim from concrete pews
the city sizzles like an anvil
'neath a blacksmith's blow.
Jehovah's Witness named Lightocompresto
swears its Armageddon.

M-16s stalk the mockingbird's shadow
back draft blisters red wagon
I peddled **Detroit News** from.
Search for Luc Kildare's spectacled face
in olive drab's high gauntlet,
dusk & a stray cat merge.

Reshuffling the year's losses
one eyed premonitions rise
smoke & mirrors outwit inferno's claw,
multiplies haberdasher's bogus claim.
Water sheds up & die in a rose.

Daddy convenes council of uncles
work boots propped 'round a two-flat stoop sunset 'n
ash torch their long shadows,
wallets weigh stop-work blues.

Lucifer night-rides bloodshot sky
flames leap a Motown block
sear hole size of Momma's faith
in the canvas awning above.

Brick don't burn but Luther Ellis holds the deed.
Empty clouds play hide & seek
suicide knob caught in Daddy's grip
powder blue Chevy swerves past embers.
What's left settles; unsettled still.

Statue At Sacred Heart Seminary: Part I

(July, 1968)

We yelped like torched dogs.
After the loot & burn
M-16s lowered, tanks retreat to 'Nam
I rushed before school
as if Judas returned
& rolled away the stone.

Face, hands, glazed coal
whitewashed & back again
three times or more, clandestine
while the salvaged sleep.
Even the alabaster foot
beyond his robe.

Woven through darkness
relentless eyes tarry
through slits of patience
black paint in trunk of a '62 Ford,
saint & soldier play shell game
with a deity in the dark.

Momma declares
its just a statue, he lives within.
I peer up at a white one
on our dining room wall
for a moment
I'm saved.

Statue At Sacred Heart Seminary: Part II

(August, 2012)

Papal lips' urgent flap
Lost Books & Nag Hamada
sealed in Easter's cadaver.
Pope John Paul visits Sacred Heart
the white statue utters prophesies
even Rome denies. Brother King coffined
in Motor City's effigy; bulletproof leather
& black berets wear defiance,
rewrite gospel one savior at a time.

If only thoughts were my tongue's taskmaster.
As a boy I transcribe on sheets of fire,
wonder why Cro-Magnon aren't in Genesis
or Coelacanthus don't dangle
from saber skin. Sixth, seventh,
forty-eighth birthday; the words
two thousand years ago echo,
time propped perfectly still
resurrection fossilized by fear.

Returning from school
I'd pass the other statue
crossed-over & cornered.
Granddaddy use to say: *Someday*
blue-eyed gatekeepers will claim
heaven's for those who pay.
Concealed behind black wrought iron
subterfuge discovered half a century late
sleight of hand outstretched like scepter.

World News Tonight

Summer, 1966

Baptized in gasoline
War weary woman
In a black robe
Ignites in silence

Martyred before smoke clears
A charred rose blooms
Buddhist nun delivered
Through Cronkite's glare

Spellbound by her peace
On our coffee table
Mother's philodendron
Recoils from heat

A family's uncounted casualty
Illuminates protest
Far too much dying
On a Thursday

Spirit northbound, the body south
Unable to reach her
& extinguish the horror
From my sleep

Thanks

To my brother Alphonso

In '64 a crate stamped **fragile**
arrives *priority* from Munich,
Nina Simone *Live At Town Hall*
grabs our Grundig by the throat.
Thanks Uncle Sam,
lands you stateside before napalm

explodes in our living room
on Six O'clock News.
Tet Offensive launched
you sip Akadama plum wine
in a paisley robe and ascot. Thanks

for punching Ford Motor's day shift
Italian sweaters I'd runway to school
shanghai splash of Jade East,
scented beyond my years
made skirts flutter
earlier than puberty in spring.

Playing football in the rain
soiled tees cling to puny torsos,
your azure Impala diamondbacks
through mid May's drizzle.
Hugging LaSalle Park's west curve
we pause, fixate on your style.
Coaxed from Marvin's *Pride & Joy*
you synchronize these ears
to *My Favorite Things*. Thanks

for your boot up my ass
as Daddy collapsed into black lung
at pace of a thousand snails.
For appearing like ramrod
swaying balance of power
between me and Rudy's blade.

Slathered on beer & nuts
at Tiger Stadium, you were there
on our side when 'Nam ended
when killing marched home fatigued.

Salty

At ninety, Momma never curses
the long hours graveyards keep.
Distilled in endless thirst
aged siblings chew teeth
Daddy gnawed to his gums.

Death only obeys the dying
Black Lung savors its calcified kill
defiance, homage to its slow burn.

Gathered to break bread
Morton's blue ocher always there
girl in downpour whispering *repent*
under a shroud of yellow umbrella,
amber & cobalt; sacred as Sabbath.

Upper lips in Kool-Aid
one eye on drumsticks
four sons bow heads,
mumble grace as steam rises
into compost of Roy's memory.

Dime store heirloom
sprinkles sea stones on cob
dipped in enough butter
so the mineral sticks,
anoint skillet fries with a dash
nearly scald my tongue.

Neck bone backslid
'cross Mississippi salt lick,
aroma got Pee-Wee & Lloyd
jus' do dropping by.

Momma's wisdom
never tallies to a child,
spoke death with eyes only
elders language I grew into
like hand-me-down suit.

Quiet as Jackson County stroll
Daddy drifts beyond his scowl
with less effort than a yawn.
Mercy leaves slivers,
solace eases the curing.

She's lamplight in a Psalter,
nephews & uncles poised to pall bear
long before his passing. Longing
drains his fading glimmer,
arthritic knees grind in prayer.

Mourning meanders like a sloth.
She plucks me from rain,
cups tempest in her palm
'til something granular turns to salve.

Most thangs be mo' savory
with a lil' sunshine.

Ain't No Mountain High Enough

Questions From My Mother

Where's the blessed woman
who picked up where I left off?

Which of you stirs
Like tornado's flame?

How could a whiskey soaked kiss
leave you so thirsty?

Who's dying hand
quenches your crave?

Will you keep oath
of yo' Daddy's tender hands

Why slumber
with swallows in your chest?

Who plants trees
swaying to your words?

Why are songs
tortured by your voice?

When will spirit
set fire to your tongue?

Where in holy psalms
Are my grand children?

Ode To Mrs. Kirk

My High School English Teacher

I am giraffe in stiletto apprehension
Couldn't hear Pushkin

Roaming bell towers in my dome
Paradise Lost eclipses the cross

Beelzebub's curse, sweet water
Fire gutting my mouth, unraveled

By *Book Of The Dead*
Ancient voices swing

Like a hypnotist's watch
Her words become torchbearers

Steppingstones lure me
Into Webster's abyss

Legends with lead wings
Hibernate on my tongue

I am salamander in flames
Ironstone simmering in her opulence

Furlough

Detroit, 1991

A lemon silk dirge
& clang of leg irons
drag apart the silence

Two jailers whisper up stone
as redwood in a corn field,
ushers Charles Edward to this sanctuary
bloodhounds would never find.
Gospel shoulda' been law
regret plummets through a hell hole
twenty seven years long, survival
blisters at the seam.

Northbound fo' poplar lost favor
Uncle Isaiah's eulogy
utters black cat deliverance.
Four boys & eight girls
moor Aunt Mariah's womb. Great
to grand savor bowls of French vanilla
we put feet in & took turns churnin'.

From a wheelchair she don't even wail,
just mourns in quiet sorrow
soothed by kinfolk grace
& first son's furlough,
shook from sleep 'neath Lucifer's weed.

I reminiscence from the third pew.
If me & cuz' could trim a spruce
splurge on cat fishin' Bear Creek,
spin forty-fives & harmless lies
as apologies drift from Smokey's lips.

I'd spot him one mo' chance
at Nine Ball for ten
look in his eyes, ask why desire
cocks the trigger with a syringe
as cell block D gnaws
like cancer in his shoe.

There's mo' to livin' than breath.
Prayer beads up in my niece's throat,
her anguish brings a turnkey to his knees.

Secrets

Consequence haunts
Infidelity's last kiss
Judges peer through keyholes
Witnessing every move

Cockroaches mock extinction
Mirrors trail the action
Revealing the irony of glass
Wife & mistress
Become last will & testament

Darkness
Eclipses the eye
Painted rock stars
Moonlight for a prince
Runaways soak up age,
Admirals at sea

Coelacanth with fire eyes
Thrown back by hungry fisherman
Whispers echo layer upon layer,
Bushmen honor ancient fish
Curators hone in, circling
Each clandestine breath

Comrades burning old flames
Step from a photograph
& reshuffle the past
A string of failures
Falls asleep at the wheel

Curtain opens; silence gives a standing O!
A hand puppet slips up the ass
Grins & goes on

Muse

sniff that wild orchid
melt insincerity's iron robe
soak your tongue in brine

wallow in mud from Komunyakaa's bayou
sip black bottom & honeysuckle
wade in Sylvia's anxiety

sleep with Pablo's red lover
swim in womb water, drown in solitude
seduced by cathedrals of language

smell it, cloaked in velvet fire
veiled in a menagerie of words
slumbering on sugared stones

glistening
like you just made love to a galaxy
now your exquisite elephant sings!

Tracks Of My Tears

Empty Graves

Peaceful as embryos, each hole
only soil & unsettled stones.
Suspended at earth's edge
the living pray their dead retire.

Undertakers bleed trust funds
pilfer mattresses, juggle gray torsos
heaped sun to subterranean room
as if rigor mortis wore shoes.

Eulogies strewn about; eyes
stick out of mud
limbs fossilize like dinosaurs,
a finger pointed south.

How could this happen?
God's landscape thawed
diggers strong & nourished,
war zone centuries removed.

Dying relinquishes slow, passing
strung cross lukewarm cemeteries
over pandemonium of nails.

Cathedrals of grass & stars wail
asking what's going on,
what's happening in mercy's tower
who's tending death's planet?

Widow's dried azalea
pressed between Revelations,
children sift through piles of cadavers.
52nd longitude opens,
Uncle's missing tattoo
a day's misery removed.

Grief undresses ritual a mother wore.
Hands at her belly rekindle sorrow
in ways the insufferable can't.

Sanctuary of flame
death's insatiable score
double-crossed, my body
ablaze like monk
fire the tomb.

Goree To Harlem

Amazing Grace___
humming north with azaleas
not even foreigners
hemorrhaging in throat
of new hemispheres.
Misery, ship's belly
bloated with flesh.

Branded: smothered in yams
whips, Bible verse & fatback
breastfed on liberty's milk 'n nails
'neath white sheet's tow.
Honey seed 'o hope sharecrops dream
as Harpo wails griot's blues
noose 'round his note.

Freedom's curse, lowdown south
Union Blue with bullet holes
trembling in your hands, desiccated rose
slug lodged in breastplate psalm.

Indigo girl name Nation
riding Safina on handlebars
of a hand-me-down Schwinn,
pink balloon thumbing spokes
dreaming through a portal
corner of 5th Ave. & 1929.

Song of every borough
leap from Harlem's abundant tongue
backlash & rhythm hiss
with fury of renaissance.

Delicious anger, cane juice joy
hang time to ragtime
trapped in cotton gins
cars & skyscrapers
hungry for spider monkeys
weaving a pinstripe web.

Permanence forged in blood & whiskey
wingtips French kiss pork bellies,
wrestle rouge women & numbers
'long Mississippi, between flag & Cosa Nostra
cross White House marble flo'.

Panic whips, bulls cower
winter's hammer
breaks Wall Street's yellow bell.
Soup lines link together
like string of pearls
floating from steamy kitchens
clear to Venus. Black Monday
spitting paper tycoons
empty handed & summoned.

All that jazz, draining spittoons
& sole dressin' boots of preying men
mirrors break for pomade & talc.
Conking those succulent locks
pompadours, six waves straight back
spit-shining steppin' fetch-it faces.

love haiku #2

long as we have breath
the mouth is the heart's prism
desire made flesh

House Broken

By a bus stop
& ten thousand rides
To fields of lilies
Just beyond ghetto gladness

River Jordan's glory
Momma tidies quarters
Fist full o' transfers
With rope burn

Filth brought home to me
From Rosa's crowded seat
Imbedded beneath nails
Of her countless arthritic fingers

About Jawanza Dumisani

A native Detroiter, Jawanza Dumisani's first full length collection of poems, *Black Raising Cane Over Red*, celebrates Detroit's magical and turbulent era with provocative fondness. From street wise game to dope house drama, his eloquent, yet gritty style transports you back in time with switch blade precision. Beautifully spun narratives weave a tapestry that plunks you smack dab in the midst of Motown gladness while sharing the intimacy of his family tree. This stunning collection is part I of a two-book project chronicling his early youth followed by *Urban Miaffa* in 2015, a photo journey documenting Detroit's current struggle to not only survive, but re-emerge from a half century of decay spawned by the civil unrest of the sixties. A perfect coffee table companion, complimented by excerpts from Jawanza's poignant verse and more. Also on Glover Lane Press.

Since joining The World Stage Anassi Writer's in 1997, Jawanza Dumisani earned a scholarship in '03 and studied with Suzanne Lummis at UCLA. In '05 he received THE PEN AWARD and was mentored by Chris Abani. He served as Director of Literary Programming at The World Stage from 2005 to 2011 and currently serves as Executive Director of Lady Between The Lines Art Agency. Following publication of his first chapbook *Stoetry* on FarStarFire Press in 2008 Jawanza Dumisani continues to garner the praise of his peers across southern California and beyond.

Visit Jawanza at http://jawanzadumisani.wix.com/jawanzadumisani

You can also visit Jawanza at Amazon.com/author/Jawanzadumisani

About Glover Lane Press

Thank you so much for your purchase of this exceptional book by Jawanza Dumisani!

We are so very honored to be the publishing house for this empowering book of poetry and haiku.

If you enjoyed reading Black Raising Cane Over Red, please visit our website for our new, featured and upcoming publications.

Azaan Kamau started Glover Lane Press in the summer of 2000 to give a voice to poets and writers worldwide. Azaan and Glover Lane Press have helped countless individuals publish and distribute media in print, audio and in digital formats.

One of Azaan's publishing goals is to focus on marginalized or over-looked communities of writers, poets, artists, and photographers. Azaan feels everyone has a story that must be heard or recorded. Another important goal for Azaan is to use the proceeds from her personal book sales to improve the lives of people around the world. Azaan's books and her companies will feed the hungry, house the homeless, heal the sick, educate and eradicate disease, etc!

www. gloverlanepress.webs.com
www.letterstomybully.webs.com
www.Facebook.com/Gloverlanepress

For an entire list of our print books and electronic books, you can also visit us on www.Amazon.com

Again, thank you for your purchase!

www.ingramcontent.com/pod-product-compliance
Lightning Source LLC
LaVergne TN
LVHW091204080426
835509LV00006B/821